Teaspoons, Tablespoons, and Cups

Holly Karapetkova

ROURKE PUBLISHING

Vero Beach, Florida 32964

www.rourkepublishing.com

PHOTO CREDITS: Title Page: © William Mahar; P. 5: © Rob Marmion; all other photos © Renee Brady

Editor: Meg Greve

Cover design by Nicola Stratford, bdpublishing.com

Interior Design by Heather Botto

Library of Congress Cataloging-in-Publication Data

Karapetkova, Holly.
  Teaspoons, tablespoons, and cups / Holly Karapetkova.
    p. cm. -- (Concept)
  ISBN 978-1-60694-381-6 (hard cover)
  ISBN 978-1-60694-513-1 (soft cover)
  ISBN 978-1-60694-571-1 (bilingual)
  1. Units of measurement--Juvenile literature. I. Title.
  QC90.6.K3687 2010
  530.8'1--dc22

                          2009016021

Printed in the USA

CG/CG

ROURKE PUBLISHING

www.rourkepublishing.com - rourke@rourkepublishing.com
Post Office Box 643328 Vero Beach, Florida 32964

Teaspoons, tablespoons, and cups help us measure amounts.

We use them when we cook.
They tell us how much we need.

The teaspoon is very small.

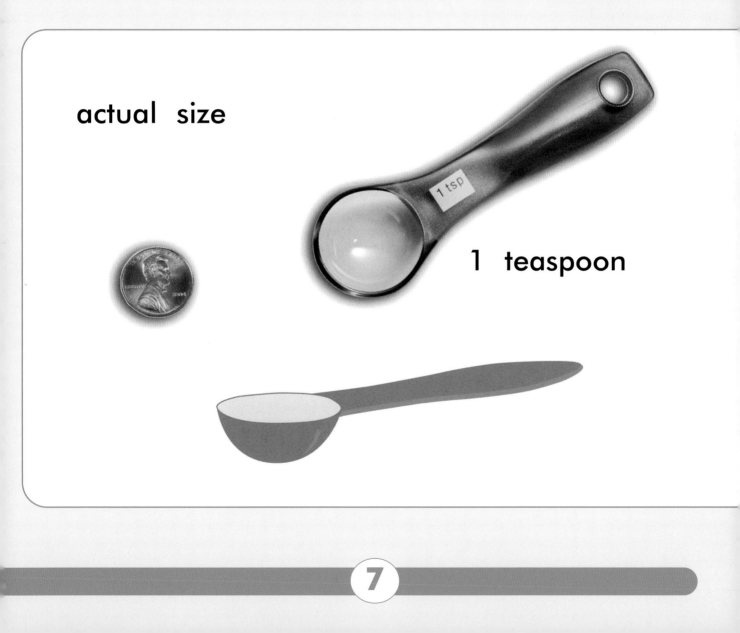

actual size

1 tsp

1 teaspoon

How much do we need?
We need one teaspoon.

Three teaspoons make
one tablespoon.

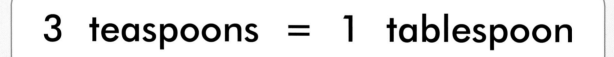

3 teaspoons = 1 tablespoon

3 teaspoons

=

1 tablespoon

How much do we need?
We need one tablespoon.

1 tablespoon

actual size

Sixteen tablespoons make one cup.

16 tablespoons = 1 cup

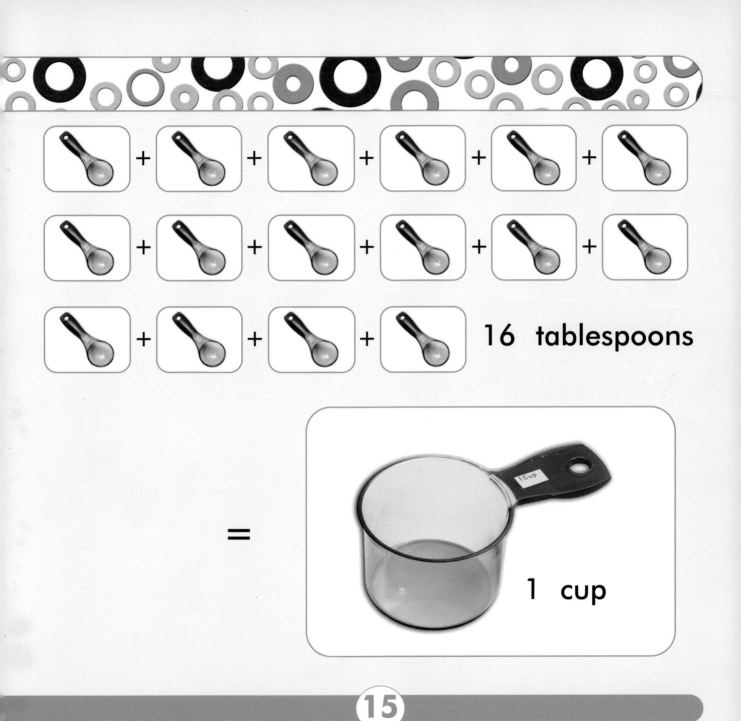

16 tablespoons

= 1 cup

How much do we need?
We need one cup.
Measure carefully.

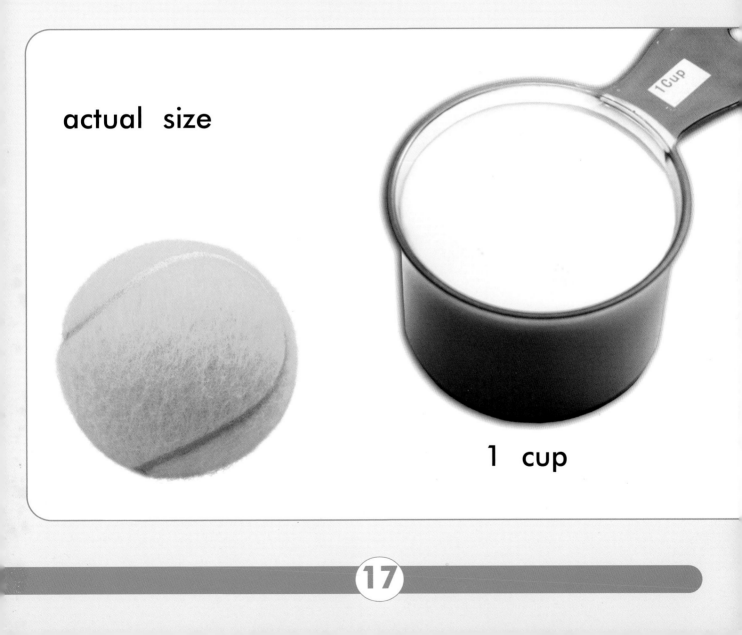

actual size

1 cup

Which one holds the largest amount?

1 tablespoon

1 teaspoon

1 cup

Which one holds the
smallest amount?

1 cup

1   tablespoon

1   teaspoon

Converting Liquid Measurements from Customary to Metric

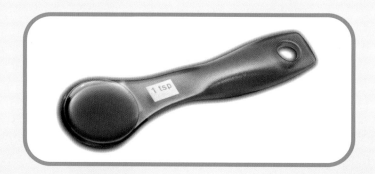

1 teaspoon = 5 milliliters
(customary) (metric)

1 **tablespoon** = 15 **milliliters**
(customary)   *(metric)*

1 **cup** = 236 **milliliters**
(customary)   *(metric)*

Index

Websites to Visit

www.mathsisfun.com/measure

www.edhelper.com/measurement.htm

www.factmonster.com/ipka/A0876863.html

www.kidsacookin.ksu.edu

www.nzmaths.co.nz/volume-and-capacity-units-work

About the Author

Holly Karapetkova, Ph.D., loves writing books and poems for kids and adults. She teaches at Marymount University and lives in the Washington, D.C., area with her son K.J. and her two dogs, Muffy and Attila.